Planning to Please

Written and Illustrated by
Ron and Rebekah Coriell

Fleming H. Revell Company
Old Tappan, New Jersey

© 1981 Fleming H. Revell Company
All rights reserved
Printed in the United States of America

Discern
fern

Able to See Things as They Really Are

But strong meat belongeth to them that are of full age, even those who by reason of use have their senses exercised to discern both good and evil.

     Hebrews 5:14

Discernment
in the Bible

Excitement stirred among those who watched the construction of the ninety-foot-high statue. But three men grew sad as the idol neared completion. They could not worship this false god. Would this mean that they would have to die for their convictions? Their names were Shadrach, Meshach, and Abed-nego.

Each of these men were Jews who had been taken to Babylon in 597 B.C. They were handsome, healthy, and intelligent. At the palace they were trained in the Babylonian arts of war, hunting, and leisure. They learned the Chaldean tongue and how to read and write the wedge-shaped cuneiform script. They also learned mathematics. Even their names were changed from Hebrew to the Babylonian language. These three and Daniel had discerned that it was wrong for them to eat meat that had been offered to idols. Instead they ate only vegetables and drank water. They grew healthy and wise until they were chosen to serve among the officials in King Nebuchadnezzar's court.

The idol was constructed in the Plain of Dura, in the Province of Babylon. Nebuchadnezzar sent messengers throughout his empire, commanding that all princes, governors, captains, judges, treasurers, counselors, sheriffs, and rulers should attend the dedication of the idol.

As the throng stood before the idol, a herald shouted out, "To you it is commanded, O people, nations, and languages, That at what time ye hear the sound of the cornet, flute, harp, sackbut, psaltery, dulcimer, and all kinds of musick, ye fall down and worship the golden image that Nebuchadnezzar the king hath set up"(Daniel 3:4, 5).

Shadrach, Meshach, and Abed-nego looked at each other in dismay. Their worst fears were realized. Until this time, they had been able to serve the Babylonians and still worship Jehovah, their God. Each man discerned that to bow to this idol would be sinful.

The herald continued, "And whoso falleth not down and worshippeth shall the same hour be cast into the midst of a burning fiery furnace" (Daniel 3:6).

Each of these Hebrew servants clearly discerned that only two choices were possible: obedience to the king and disobedience to Jehovah, or obedience to Jehovah and certain death in the fiery furnace.

As the music began to play, they made their decision. All three chose to stand for Jehovah God.

Thousands fell with faces to the ground and hands outstretched in humble worship. Almost like statues themselves, the three men stood quietly until the music stopped and everyone rose to their feet.

Their stand did not go unnoticed. Certain Chaldeans immediately went before the king and accused the Jews of disloyalty.

Nebuchadnezzar was insulted and enraged. Angrily he summoned the three Hebrews to appear before him to explain their actions.

"Is it true, O Shadrach, Meshach, and Abed-nego?" asked the king. "Do not ye serve my gods, nor worship the golden image which I have set up?" (Daniel 3:14).

Before they could answer, he told them that he was going to give them a second chance. He would instruct the musicians to play again, and this time they must fall down and worship his idol. If not, he asked them, "And who is that God that shall deliver you out of my hands?" (Daniel 3:15).

Again the three Hebrews clearly saw their predicament. But their resolve to obey their God was firm.

They said, "O Nebuchadnezzar .... If it be so, our God whom we serve is able to deliver us from the burning fiery furnace, and He will deliver us out of thine hand, O king. But if not, be it known unto thee, O king, that we will not serve thy gods, nor worship the golden image which thou hast set up" (Daniel 3:16–18).

Anger swelled within Nebuchadnezzar. These Hebrew slaves were defying him to his face. Turning to an aide, he ordered that the fire in the large smelting furnace be heated seven times hotter than usual. Then he commanded some of the strongest men in his army to bind Shadrach, Meshach, and Abed-nego and to throw them into the furnace.

Court officials mocked and yelled at the Hebrews as they were taken from the palace. The crowd followed the soldiers, anxious to see justice done.

The furnace was a large pit dug out of the ground, with steep walls on all sides. It was used to melt metals and for executing criminals.

Waves of heat radiated toward the crowd. They had to stop far from the opening of the furnace. But the soldiers had their orders. They had to press on with their victims until they could cast them into the flames. They moved forward bravely until the soldiers were able to push the Hebrews into the pit opening. But before they could retreat, the heat engulfed them. All three soldiers died.

Nebuchadnezzar had come to watch the execution. As he sat on his throne, he was amazed to see figures walking in the midst of the furnace, where the fire was the hottest.

Jumping up, he pointed and spoke, "Did not we cast three men bound into the midst of the fire? ... Lo, I see four men loose, walking in the midst of the fire, and they have no hurt; and the form of the fourth is like the Son of God" (Daniel 3:24, 25).

Coming closer to the furnace, the king cupped his hands to his mouth and shouted, "Shadrach, Meshach, and Abed-nego, ye servants of the most high God, come forth, and come hither" (Daniel 3:26).

A cry of astonishment rose from the crowd as the three Hebrews ascended out of the pit. Amazingly, their bodies were not blackened; their hair was not singed; nor was there a smell of smoke in their clothes!

Then Nebuchadnezzar spoke: "Blessed be the God of Shadrach, Meshach, and Abed-nego, who hath sent His angel, and delivered His servants that trusted in Him, and have changed the king's word, and yielded their bodies, that they might not serve nor worship any god, except their own God" (Daniel 3:28).

Then the king warned that anyone who spoke against Jehovah God would be cut in pieces and that their houses would be made refuse heaps. The king also promoted these three servants to higher positions in the Province of Babylon.

God was pleased with the discernment of his servants Shadrach, Meshach, and Abed-nego. Because they clearly saw the choices that were before them in their time of crisis, they were able to stand for God and win the respect of a pagan king.

The story of Shadrach, Meshach, and Abed-nego is taken from Daniel 1:8-1:21;3:1-30.

Discernment
of a Hero of the Faith

A man of discernment is one who can see things as they really are, oftentimes in spite of conflicting messages. Such were the times during the founding days of our country. A man who was known for his discernment was a pastor named John Witherspoon.

In the fifteen years Reverend Witherspoon pastored in Scotland, he became well-known as a speaker and author. After earning a Doctor of Divinity degree at the University of Aberdeen, he became a recognized leader of the Church of Scotland.

Dr. Witherspoon was called to America to assume the presidency of Princeton University. Yet as great as the need was at Princeton, the circumstances of the times soon provided John Witherspoon with an additional calling. The Colonies were wrestling under the burdensome dictates of England. Debates were raging about independence. These were times that demanded a man with Dr. Witherspoon's leadership abilities and discernment.

Dr. Witherspoon was sent to join the Colonial Assembly of New Jersey. Later he participated in the convention that framed the first constitution of New Jersey. Sensing his wise, discerning spirit, his constituency asked him to serve as a delegate to the Continental Congress, which penned the Declaration of Independence.

Early in the Colonies' contest with England, Dr. Witherspoon clearly discerned the truth about the mother country. England forbade the Colonies to buy, sell, ship, or manufacture goods under profitable conditions. They were also being unfairly taxed. John Witherspoon denounced the acts of that government as "unjust, impolitic, and barbarous." In 1774, on behalf of New Jersey, he prepared a memorial to the first Continental Congress, declaring that the claim of the British Parliament was "illegal and unconstitutional." He added that, "We are firmly determined never to submit to it and do deliberately prefer war, with all its horrors, and even extermination itself, to slavery riveted on us and our posterity."

Dr. Witherspoon clearly saw that liberty from the dictates of England was the only pathway for the Colonies if they wished to prosper as people. When the Continental Congress was discussing whether or not the times were ripe for action, John Witherspoon interrrupted forcefully, "Ripe? If you do not soon act, they will be rotten!"

When at last the Declaration of Independence was signed, Reverend Witherspoon was the only minister of the Gospel to sign it. In fact he was the only minister who ever sat in the Continental Congress.

Besides being a delegate to the Congress, he served on many powerful committees—a testimony to the trust that others placed in his wise discernment of the issues. As a member of the Ways and Means Committee, John Witherspoon opposed the use of paper currency. He warned, "If you are going to have armies, you must pay them with money, real money, not imitation money"; and, "If you were going to pay them with real money, you must have an organization of states ... in which you could levy taxes and get them." Thus Reverend Witherspoon wisely discerned the need for hard cash—gold or silver coin—a solid union of states, and taxes.

During the ups and downs of the revolutionary war, Reverend Witherspoon was a staunch supporter of General George Washington. As Washington experienced defeat in battles, some in the Congress spoke of compromising with the English. Reverend Witherspoon always hotly denounced such notions. He declared once, "I would favor continuing the contest, even were the state of affairs ten times more hopeless." After the war, a British writer wrote that "this political firebrand ... had no less share in the Revolution than had Washington himself." It was a fitting tribute to Reverend Witherspoon's energies and discerning service on behalf of his country.

After the war, he resumed active work at Princeton, and during the last two years of his life, he was blind. But with the aid of a college student as secretary, he continued to prepare and to deliver sermons. Reverend Witherspoon said, "There are some persons who give away so much wisdom in their speech that they leave none behind to govern their actions." Such advice proved that his discerning spirit had not left him, even in old age.

On November 15, 1794, Reverend Witherspoon died. His life was used by God at a time in our country's history when a man of discernment was most needed.

Character Development Challenges

Discerning Good and Evil

Solomon prayed, "Give therefore thy servant an understanding heart to judge thy people, that I may discern between good and bad" (1 Kings 3:9).

Look up each Scripture reference listed below and discern what is good and evil. Write the answer in the space provided.

GOOD
1. Psalms 73:28 _____
2. Psalms 92: 1, 2 _____
3. Psalms 112:5 _____
4. Psalms 119:39 _____
5. Psalms 119:71 _____
6. Psalms 113:1 _____
7. Proverbs 16:20 _____
8. Proverbs 17:22 _____
9. Lamentations 3:26 _____
10. Lamentations 3:27 _____
11. 1 Timothy 2:1-3 _____
12. Proverbs 12:25 _____
13. Proverbs 15:23 _____
14. Psalms 147:1 _____
15. Psalms 34:8 _____

EVIL
1. John 3:20 _____
2. 1 Corinthians 15:33 _____
3. Ephesians 4:31 _____
4. 1 Thessalonians 5:22 _____
5. 1 Timothy 6:20 _____
6. Hebrews 3:12 _____
7. James 3:8 _____
8. James 4:16 _____
9. Proverbs 15:28 _____
10. Jeremiah 2:19 _____
11. Galatians 1:3, 4 _____
12. James 4:17 _____
13. Proverbs 2:12 _____
14. Proverbs 6:24 _____
15. Proverbs 12:20 _____

Order
mortar

Everything in Its Place

Let all things be done
decently and in order.
    1 Corinthians 14:40

Orderliness in the Bible

Gloom overshadowed the city of Jerusalem. Wicked King Ahaz had died, leaving a trail of terror and tragedy. During his reign, a foreign nation had plundered the land, killing 120,000 men and capturing 200,000 men, women, and children. In order to buy protection, Ahaz had given away treasures in the house of the Lord and had closed its doors. He also worshiped the idols of his oppressors. People feared that the end of the nation of Judah was at hand.

Hezekiah, Ahaz's son, was twenty-five years old when he began to reign. In his years of training, he had been taught by the great prophet Isaiah. Isaiah had instructed Hezekiah to love the true God, Jehovah. Therefore in the first month of his reign, Hezekiah commanded that the doors of the house of the Lord be opened.

On an inspection tour, the king sadly noted the disorderliness and filthiness of the Temple. He called the Levite priests together so that he could address them.

He said, "Hear me, ye Levites, sanctify now yourselves, and sanctify the house of the Lord God of your fathers, and carry forth the filthiness out of the holy place" (2 Chronicles 29:5).

He told them that the sufferings of Judah and Jerusalem had been caused by the sins of their fathers. Hezekiah then promised that he was going to do all that he could to see that the wrath of God abated, and he would help the people to once again deserve God's blessing.

Excitement filled the hearts of the people who had long hoped for a revival. Eagerly the priests returned to their homes to gather the necessary tools to begin restoring the Temple.

Hezekiah insisted that everything be done in an orderly way. Their efforts must be in accordance with the ancient laws that God had given Moses. Therefore the priests went through the ritual of cleansing themselves. They came with clean clothes, and as they arrived at the Temple, they carefully washed their hands and feet. This symbolized their clean hearts toward God.

They worked diligently, removing all the broken utensils and furniture. Walls were scrubbed, and the floors were swept. When all the refuse was collected, it was carried outside the city and thrown into a ravine called the Kidron. This valley served as the city dump. It took sixteen days to finish the cleansing of the Temple.

Upon its completion, Hezekiah ordered all the rulers of Jerusalem to gather with him at the house of the Lord. They brought with them seven bulls, seven rams, and seven he goats. These animals were slain and offered on the altar as sacrifices to God for the sins of the nation. At the same time, 4,000 Levites stood nearby, singing and playing cymbals, harps, and trumpets, in praise to God.

Then Hezekiah commanded that offerings of thanksgiving be made and freewill burnt offerings be reinstated. So great was the outpouring of the people's worship that 70 bulls, 100 rams, and 200 lambs were freely offered. In addition, 600 oxen and 3,000 sheep, as well as many other kinds of offerings, were brought as holy gifts. So it was that the Temple was restored to service and the sacrifices offered again. Hezekiah and all the people were filled with gladness because of what God had so quickly helped them accomplish.

The Passover was one of the most important celebrations of the Jews. However, they had not practiced this annual event since the days of King Solomon, many years before. Hezekiah knew that for God to be fully pleased with His nation, they must return to the observance of all celebrations commanded in the laws of Moses. Therefore, throughout the land, he sent invitations for the people to come to Jerusalem to celebrate the Passover. Although some of the unrepentant people laughed and scorned the invitation, many humbled themselves and came.

In preparation for this gathering, the people of Jerusalem searched the city for heathen altars and idols. These were knocked down and taken to the dump at Kidron.

So great was the seven-day celebration that it was extended another seven days. King Hezekiah gave the people 1,000 young bulls and 7,000 sheep for offerings. The princes donated 1,000 young bulls and 10,000 sheep. All who attended were filled with great joy, and the Lord heard their prayers.

To continue his return to godliness, Hezekiah began a massive campaign against idol worship. The people went into the surrounding countryside in search of idol altars, obelisks, and heathen centers of worship. When found, these were torn down and burned. The king also reorganized the priests and Levites into service corps to offer the daily burnt offerings and peace offerings and to worship and give thanks and praise to God. In addition he required that the people once again begin to pay tithes to the priests and Levites. With this income they would not need outside employment. Instead they could devote all their energies to serving in the Temple.

The people responded immediately and generously. Wine, oil, honey, and grain were brought and laid in great piles. Some brought cattle and sheep.

Hezekiah was amazed when he saw the massive tithes. Azariah, the high priest, told him that there was more than enough for the needs of the priests and Levites. They didn't know what to do with the surplus. So the king ordered that storerooms be prepared in the Temple and that the tithes be stored in an orderly fashion.

A genealogical register of all the priests and Levites was begun so that records could be kept indicating those who were to receive regular food allotments. Special priests were assigned to issue these foods and other supplies to the priests who served the people in outlying towns.

Hezekiah was one of the few godly kings in the declining years of the nation of Judah. He worked very hard to encourage a new respect for the Temple, the law, and godly living. Orderliness was one of the character traits that helped him to accomplish his goals.

The story of Hezekiah is taken from 2 Chronicles 28:16-31:21.

Orderliness
of a Hero of the Faith

Someone has said, "Birds of a feather flock together." Although this saying may be true in many cases, it was not applicable in the courtship and marriage of Jonathan and Sarah Edwards.

No one would have thought that they were right for each other. Jonathan was a brilliant young college graduate of twenty when he began to court Sarah. She was only thirteen. Courtship at such an early age was not unusual in the 1700s, due to the fact that the life expectancy of a woman was about thirty-three years.

Jonathan was an untypically tall man: He stood over six feet. He was also moody, clumsy, very poor at conversation, and very shy. Sarah was cheerful and vibrant, with erect posture and excellent manners. She had the ability to talk to anyone and keep his or her interest.

At first Sarah was afraid of Jonathan. But as he continued to show an interest in her, she began to sense that there was a sensitive, interesting man behind his awkwardness. Due to the unusual amount of education Sarah received from her wealthy parents, she and Jonathan shared an interest in books and in the study of nature. Sarah's father was also impressed with Jonathan's graduate work at Yale College. He saw a promising future for young Edwards. Sarah kept Jonathan waiting three years before she at last agreed to marry him.

Sarah Edwards possessed the character trait of orderliness. Upon the completion of their clapboard house in Northampton, Massachusetts, she purposed to make it a tidy, comfortable, and enjoyable home. Many people ate from wooden bowls; the Edwards family ate from pewter dishes. She grew a little plot of cooking herbs near the kitchen door. This made it handy to garnish a bland dish of food with parsley, spearmint, or sage. Sarah was thoughtful in the little details of life, such as taking an extra moment to stamp a design on a block of home-churned butter. She even took the time to tie her hair with a ribbon before she made her appearance at breakfast. Outside the house she planted day lilies, hollyhocks, pansies, and pinks.

Jonathan had the thrifty habit of saving used paper. He would write horizontally and then vertically on the pages of his diary. Sarah helped him save paper by keeping old bills and shopping lists and then stitching them together into handmade notebooks. When Jonathan became a minister, he wrote his sermons in these notebooks, on the back of the bills.

So orderly did Sarah keep the Edwards' home that they were always ready for company. The inns of the day were often vile and dangerous places in which to lodge. Therefore traveling clergy would carefully time their journeys so that they were in the vicinity of the Edwards' home at nightfall. Sarah's generous hospitality would turn none away.

Most people rose early in those days, because their routine was timed by the clockwork of the farm. Jonathan awakened even earlier than the farmers, because he believed that each moment was sacred and must be well spent. Therefore Sarah was in the habit of awakening the household before sunrise. They began with prayers by candlelight. Then they all heard a chapter read from the Bible and asked God's blessing on the day.

Sarah supervised the planting of the garden and the instructing of the hired man with his daily work. Reverend Edwards once asked, "Isn't it about time the hay was cut?" Sarah is said to have mildly replied, "It's been in the barn for two weeks."

The Edwardses had eleven children. Large families were common in those days, and Sarah's orderliness was mirrored in all eleven. Sarah assigned chores, so that everyone had work to complete. One child made tea, while another brought in wood. Someone would pack a lunch for a guest, and another brother or sister set the table. There was the cooking roast to be watched, as well as the fire, which was kept burning twenty-four hours a day. The house functioned efficiently because the whole family was taught the importance of orderliness and the joy of working together.

The Edwardses also encouraged their children to be careful with their money. The family Bible contained an orderly record of the savings of each child, with receipts, expenditures, and debts neatly recorded.

Perhaps Sarah's greatest contribution to her husband was her ability to keep their large household running in such order. Jonathan Edwards was then able to devote many hours to study as he preached, pastored, and wrote his way into American history.

Character Development Challenges

Developing the Habits of Orderliness

It has been said that it takes six weeks to form a habit. Developing the character trait of orderliness requires good habits. Below is a list of projects. Mark each task as it is accomplished. Six weeks later, orderliness should become habit if each task has been performed faithfully.

Orderliness Projects	Week One	Week Two	Week Three	Week Four	Week Five	Week Six
Daily devotions	▫▫▫▫▫▫▫	▫▫▫▫▫▫▫	▫▫▫▫▫▫▫	▫▫▫▫▫▫▫	▫▫▫▫▫▫▫	▫▫▫▫▫▫▫
Orderly devotional notebook	▫▫▫▫▫▫▫	▫▫▫▫▫▫▫	▫▫▫▫▫▫▫	▫▫▫▫▫▫▫	▫▫▫▫▫▫▫	▫▫▫▫▫▫▫
Weekly offering given to God	▫▫▫▫▫▫▫	▫▫▫▫▫▫▫	▫▫▫▫▫▫▫	▫▫▫▫▫▫▫	▫▫▫▫▫▫▫	▫▫▫▫▫▫▫
Prayer before each meal	▫▫▫▫▫▫▫	▫▫▫▫▫▫▫	▫▫▫▫▫▫▫	▫▫▫▫▫▫▫	▫▫▫▫▫▫▫	▫▫▫▫▫▫▫
Scheduling the day's events	▫▫▫▫▫▫▫	▫▫▫▫▫▫▫	▫▫▫▫▫▫▫	▫▫▫▫▫▫▫	▫▫▫▫▫▫▫	▫▫▫▫▫▫▫
Making the bed	▫▫▫▫▫▫▫	▫▫▫▫▫▫▫	▫▫▫▫▫▫▫	▫▫▫▫▫▫▫	▫▫▫▫▫▫▫	▫▫▫▫▫▫▫
Orderly closet	▫▫▫▫▫▫▫	▫▫▫▫▫▫▫	▫▫▫▫▫▫▫	▫▫▫▫▫▫▫	▫▫▫▫▫▫▫	▫▫▫▫▫▫▫
Sweeping the bedroom	▫▫▫▫▫▫▫	▫▫▫▫▫▫▫	▫▫▫▫▫▫▫	▫▫▫▫▫▫▫	▫▫▫▫▫▫▫	▫▫▫▫▫▫▫
Dusting the room	▫▫▫▫▫▫▫	▫▫▫▫▫▫▫	▫▫▫▫▫▫▫	▫▫▫▫▫▫▫	▫▫▫▫▫▫▫	▫▫▫▫▫▫▫
Putting away soiled clothes	▫▫▫▫▫▫▫	▫▫▫▫▫▫▫	▫▫▫▫▫▫▫	▫▫▫▫▫▫▫	▫▫▫▫▫▫▫	▫▫▫▫▫▫▫
Polishing shoes	▫▫▫▫▫▫▫	▫▫▫▫▫▫▫	▫▫▫▫▫▫▫	▫▫▫▫▫▫▫	▫▫▫▫▫▫▫	▫▫▫▫▫▫▫
Hanging up clothes	▫▫▫▫▫▫▫	▫▫▫▫▫▫▫	▫▫▫▫▫▫▫	▫▫▫▫▫▫▫	▫▫▫▫▫▫▫	▫▫▫▫▫▫▫
Emptying the trash	▫▫▫▫▫▫▫	▫▫▫▫▫▫▫	▫▫▫▫▫▫▫	▫▫▫▫▫▫▫	▫▫▫▫▫▫▫	▫▫▫▫▫▫▫
Helping in the kitchen	▫▫▫▫▫▫▫	▫▫▫▫▫▫▫	▫▫▫▫▫▫▫	▫▫▫▫▫▫▫	▫▫▫▫▫▫▫	▫▫▫▫▫▫▫
Orderly garage	▫▫▫▫▫▫▫	▫▫▫▫▫▫▫	▫▫▫▫▫▫▫	▫▫▫▫▫▫▫	▫▫▫▫▫▫▫	▫▫▫▫▫▫▫
Comb hair	▫▫▫▫▫▫▫	▫▫▫▫▫▫▫	▫▫▫▫▫▫▫	▫▫▫▫▫▫▫	▫▫▫▫▫▫▫	▫▫▫▫▫▫▫
Brush teeth	▫▫▫▫▫▫▫	▫▫▫▫▫▫▫	▫▫▫▫▫▫▫	▫▫▫▫▫▫▫	▫▫▫▫▫▫▫	▫▫▫▫▫▫▫
Orderly school locker or desk	▫▫▫▫▫▫▫	▫▫▫▫▫▫▫	▫▫▫▫▫▫▫	▫▫▫▫▫▫▫	▫▫▫▫▫▫▫	▫▫▫▫▫▫▫
School assignments written neatly	▫▫▫▫▫▫▫	▫▫▫▫▫▫▫	▫▫▫▫▫▫▫	▫▫▫▫▫▫▫	▫▫▫▫▫▫▫	▫▫▫▫▫▫▫

Self-Control
bowl

Doing Something
Even When I Don't Feel Like It

And every man that striveth
for the mastery is temperate
in all things. . . .
                   1 Corinthians 9:25

Self-Control
in the Bible

Queen Esther heard the wailing man's voice echoing off the walls that surrounded the public courtyard. It was Mordecai, her cousin, and he had a sad story to tell. In eleven months all the Jews in Persia were to be slaughtered. Esther and Mordecai were Jews, and this condemned them to death on the appointed day. The chain of events that brought about this crisis had begun nine years earlier.

The Persian king, Ahasuerus, decided to give a series of banquets. During the six-month period, vast numbers of oxen, game, and fowl were consumed. Those in attendance with the king included his court officials, his harem, and his bodyguards, consisting of 14,000 persons. Also summoned to the banquets were the governors of surrounding provinces, army chiefs, and nobles. When these days were finished, an additional feast of seven days was proclaimed for all the population of the Persian capital of Shushan.

Wine was plentiful, and men drank until they were drunk. It was in this state that Ahasuerus decided to display the beauty of his favorite wife, Queen Vashti. He commanded seven of his servants to call the queen. But Vashti refused. It was against the custom of the Persians for women to appear unveiled in public.

Ahasuerus was enraged at the embarrassing disobedience of his wife. He was told by counselors that Vashti must be banished and a new queen sought for him. This plan pleased the king, and immediately a search for beautiful young girls was begun throughout the empire. This process lasted four years.

One of the young girls selected to compete was a Jewish orphan named Esther. Her cousin, Mordecai, had raised her as if she were his own daughter.

Most girls would be glad to become queen. But Esther was a young woman who loved God, and she knew the wickedness of King Ahasuerus. It must have taken great self-control to accept her selection as a candidate.

The maidens were housed at the palace for one year in order to undergo the proper preparations before being presented to the king. At the end of this time, Esther was selected as his favorite. The royal crown was placed on her head, and she was given the position among the royal wives formerly held by Vashti.

After this time, Ahasuerus promoted a man named Haman to be his prime minister. According to tradition, this man was of the royal race of the Amalekites—the bitter enemies of the Jews. Everyone honored him because of his high position. As he passed by the gate to the palace, all who were nearby would bow low to the ground. But Mordecai, the Jew, refused to bow. When this was reported to Haman, he was insulted and angered.

As he thought upon this, Haman decided that the best way to get rid of Mordecai was to kill all the Jews in the empire. At the appropriate time, when the king was full of wine, Haman presented his devious plan.

He said, "There is a certain people scattered abroad and dispersed among the people ... and their laws are diverse from all people; neither keep they the king's laws: therefore, it is not for the king's profit to suffer them. If it please the king, let it be written that they may be destroyed" (Esther 3:8, 9).

The king did not know that his beloved Esther was a Jew. Mordecai had instructed her to keep it a secret, for fear that this would prevent her from being chosen as queen. Thus, in his drunkenness, Ahasuerus saw no reason to deny Haman his request. The king took his ring from his hand and gave it to Haman, saying, "Do with them as it seemeth good to thee" (Esther 3:11).

Quickly Haman called for scribes, who wrote down his instructions and copied them many times and in many languages. These decrees were spread throughout the Persian Empire by a system of messengers. These men rode hard for fourteen miles to royal outposts, changed horses, and rode to the next station. In this way official news spread quickly.

It was upon learning this dreadful news that Mordecai put on sackcloth and ashes and went among his people, wailing. Esther soon learned of her cousin's grief and sent clothes for him to wear. He refused. Then Esther sent a servant to find out the reason for Mordecai's strange actions. Mordecai informed the servant in detail of Haman's murderous plan. He gave him a copy of the decree to give to Esther. He urged her to go before the king and beg for the lives of the Jews.

Esther sent word to Mordecai: "All the king's servants, and the people of the king's provinces, do know, that whosoever, whether man or woman, shall come unto the king into the inner court, who is not called, there is one law of his to put him to death, except such to whom the king shall hold out the golden sceptre, that he may live: but I have not been called to come in unto the king these thirty days" (Esther 4:11).

Then Mordecai warned her that she would die along with the rest of the Jews. He suggested that perhaps God had made her queen so that she could save her people.

Esther had a difficult decision to make. She did not want to go to the king, for fear that he might disapprove of her uninvited presence and have her killed. Yet she knew that the only hope for the Jews was in her intercession before Ahasuerus. Using great self-control, she agreed to try to see the king.

Prior to going, she asked that the Jews pray and fast for her for three days. Then she dressed in her finest robes and cautiously appeared in the inner court, where the king could see her. Would her husband be in a bad mood? He had not called her for thirty days. Was he angry with her? Would he be insulted by her boldness to see him? Would he get rid of her as easily as he had Vashti?

It was with great relief that she saw the scepter extended toward her. With a smile he motioned for her to come to him. "What wilt thou, queen Esther? and what is thy request? it shall be even given thee to the half of the kingdom" (Esther 5:3).

Esther reverently asked that the king and Haman come to a banquet she was preparing for them. Delighted, Ahasuerus accepted her invitation and sent word to Haman.

On the appointed day, Esther could not bring herself to tell the king about Haman. So she invited the two men to a second banquet on the next day. It was then that she gained control of herself and told her husband about Haman's wicked plan.

Ahasuerus was shocked and enraged. He learned that Haman had constructed a seventy-foot-high gallows on which to hang Mordecai. The king ordered that the wicked prime minister be hanged there instead.

The Jews were saved from destruction on the assigned day. Mordecai was promoted to prime minister, and the whole city of Shushan rejoiced. It was Esther's self-control in a time of crisis that was used by God to rescue His people.

The story of Esther is taken from the Book of Esther.

Self-Control
of a Hero of the Faith

Billy Sunday, "the baseball evangelist," was the most famous preacher of the early twentieth century. What marked his ministry was his ability to discern the sinfulness of the times and to tell people what the Bible had to say.

To many who attended his meetings, Billy was God's messenger. To others, he was a religious fanatic, a curiosity, and a free sideshow. But wherever Billy went, God moved in a mighty way.

William Ashley Sunday was born in 1862 in Ames, Iowa. His father was serving as an enlisted man in the Iowa Volunteer Infantry at the time of his son's birth. One month later, he died in an army-camp epidemic.

Billy's mother was destitute. When she realized that she could not support her family, she sent Billy to an orphanage in Davenport, Iowa. There he received an elementary education and began to show his great ability in sports.

Billy loved baseball. Because of his great speed, he soon became the sensation of the Iowa baseball diamonds. Although he was not an outstanding hitter, his spectacular fielding and aggressive running on the base paths more than made up for it. Soon he was playing with a championship, semiprofessional team in central Iowa.

It happened that the most famous professional baseball player of that era, Adrian "Cap" Anson of the Chicago White Stockings, was a native of Iowa. His aunt told him about young Sunday and persuaded him to give him a tryout. Anson did and was amazed when Billy outran one of his players, who was reputed to be the fastest in the National League. Billy was immediately placed on the roster.

Mr. Sunday became one of the best baseball players of that era. He was the first man to circle the bases in fourteen seconds. In a single season of 116 games, he stole 94 bases, 2 less than Ty Cobb's record. The best batting average of his career was .350, with a lifetime average of .257. Along with his prowess on the field came fame and success.

On his day off from work, Billy and some of his teammates were drinking heavily at a saloon in Chicago. They left the bar and clustered across the street from a group of street musicians and preachers. The group had come from the famous Old Lighthouse: the Pacific Garden Mission, on South State Street. As Billy listened, the Holy Spirit began to convict him about his sins.

Billy accepted an invitation to services at the mission, even though he was scorned by his teammates. After attending frequently, Billy gave his life to Christ in 1887.

Mr. Sunday was determined to be a personal example to everyone, showing that a professional athlete can also be a Christian gentleman. Opportunities to speak came, and he was well received by those who heard him.

He became active in a church and met and married Helen A. Thompson, who later became known as the beloved Ma Sunday. It was she who influenced her husband to give up his baseball career.

In a short period of time, Mr. Sunday was offered two outstanding tributes. He was chosen to make a world tour, but he had an injured knee and refused the honor. Then he was offered a contract of $500 per month to play for the Philadelphia Athletics. This was fabulous money in the 1890s. It took a great deal of self-control to resist the lucrative offer from Philadelphia. Mr. Sunday enjoyed the thrill of the game and the roar of the crowd, but he also realized that as a Christian he must obey God's will above all else.

The Chicago YMCA had been pressing him to join its staff as a member of the Religious Department. Billy and Ma spent much time in prayer about God's will for their lives. At last they discerned that God was leading them to work with the YMCA. His monthly salary would be $83.33.

This was a crucial decision for Billy. His ability to see God's will for his life at this juncture set the stage for a lifetime of greater service for God.

Mr. Sunday's work with the YMCA involved counseling, organizing Bible studies, and witnessing to derelicts on Skid Row. Soon he was chosen by evangelist Dr. J. Wilbur Chapman to be his campaign organizer.

For three years, Billy learned how to do everything from erecting tents to preaching. But when Dr. Chapman retired from evangelism to return to a pastorate, Billy was left without a job.

Then a telegram arrived inviting him to hold a series of meetings in

Garner, Iowa. God blessed Billy in a wonderful way. About 268 people accepted Christ. From then on, speaking invitations flooded in. Until his death in 1935, he was never without an opportunity to preach.

Billy Sunday saw drunkenness and loose morals on every hand. He purposed to tell people how wicked they were. Billy hated the devil and sin with a passion. He began an all-out warfare on both.

He said, "I'm against sin. I'll kick it as long as I've got a foot, and I'll fight it as long as I've got a fist. I'll butt it as long as I've got a head. I'll bite it as long as I've got a tooth. And when I'm old and fistless and footless and toothless, I'll gum it till I go home to Glory and it goes home to perdition!"

Mr. Sunday quickly became such a popular attraction that special, inexpensive wood tabernacles were built to house the crowds. These were constructed all over the Midwest and seated approximately 1,000 people.

Soon the "baseball evangelist" was speaking in places such as Philadelphia, Baltimore, and New York City, to crowds of 25,000 each night. In the Philadelphia meetings Mr. Sunday spoke to more than 2 million people. Over 40,000 people made decisions for Christ. In Baltimore 96,000 heard him speak in four services. Of this number, 1,843 were saved. In ten weeks of meetings in New York, almost 100,000 conversions were recorded: over 7,000 on the final day alone. In Mr. Sunday's thirty-nine years of preaching, it is reported that he addressed 100 million men and women face-to-face, without the benefit of public-address systems, radio, or television.

Billy's preaching was a mixture of humor and preaching that caused his listeners to be attentive. For example, he said, "Come on, you forces of iniquity ... come on, you assassins of character; come on, you defamers of God and enemies of the church; come on, you bull-necked, beetle-browed, hog-jowled, peanut-brained, weazel-eyed, four-flushers, false alarms, and excess baggage. In the name of God, I challenge and defy you."

Cities were never the same after Billy left them. In one city alone, 200 saloons closed down. Church attendance and membership immediately went up. One city newspaper reported that two years after a series of meetings, 83 percent of all Billy's converts were still active in Christian service.

There is no doubt that Billy Sunday was the greatest evangelist of the early twentieth century. He used self-control to choose God's will for his life. It unlocked the opportunity for Billy to play in a greater contest—one against the devil and sin.

Character Development Challenges

Who Used Self-Control?

Read the examples below. They indicate people who had the opportunity to use self-control. Some were successful and some failed. Write the person's name and whether or not he used self-control.

	Yes/No	Name
I fought a host of Midianities with only 300 men. Judges 7:1-22	_____	_____
I witnessed to Nineveh after being swallowed by a whale. Jonah 3:1-10	_____	_____
I revealed the secret of my strength. Judges 16:4-21	_____	_____
I went up into a mountain to kill my son. Genesis 22:1-13	_____	_____
I went to a witch to get counsel. 1 Samuel 28:4-7	_____	_____
I allowed a man to be stoned so that I could have his vineyard. 1 Kings 21:1-14	_____	_____
I risked my life to come uninvited before the king. Esther 4:10-16	_____	_____
I lied and said that I did not know Jesus. Matthew 26:69-75	_____	_____
I bathed in the Jordan River to get rid of my disease. 2 Kings 5:1-14	_____	_____
We told the Jews that the siege of Jerusalem was over. 2 Kings 7:3-9	_____	_____
I took the reward that was offered to the prophet. 2 Kings 5:15-27	_____	_____
I refused to curse God for all of the misfortune that I suffered. Job 2:1-10	_____	_____
I was to be God's spokesman to His people in Egypt. Exodus 4:1-16	_____	_____
I told my people to surrender to the enemy. Jeremiah 38:1-18	_____	_____
I worked fourteen years for my wife. Genesis 29:16-30	_____	_____